4 Steps to the Future:

A Quick and Clean Guide to Creating Foresight

By Richard A. K. Lum

FutureScribe

Honolulu - Anchorage - Boston - Oxford

A FutureScribe book
Published by Vision Foresight Strategy LLC

Published in the United States by Vision Foresight Strategy LLC, Honolulu.

FutureScribe is a trademark of Vision Foresight Strategy LLC.

Indexing by J. Naomi Linzer Indexing Services

ISBN: 978-0-9972783-0-9

www.visionforesightstrategy.com

This book is dedicated to James A. Dator.

Trailblazer, teacher, and guide.

Table of Contents

Preface

This book is for those times when you don't have $50,000 to spend on a big foresight or planning project, but you really want to add some structure to how your organization is thinking about that whopping uncertainty we call "the future." Whether your organization is simply confronting an uncomfortable set of new potential disruptions or if it has just experienced a big leadership change and needs to formulate a new direction, this book will provide you with the quickest yet most complete approach to systematically thinking about the future.

This book does not represent the entire range or depth of what can be done with *foresight*, but it will take you from A to Z, from having no clear, shared understanding of the future to having a new set of goals informed by critical thinking about your organization's future. And while this book isn't going to make anyone a "master" at this stuff, it will definitely make you more comfortable with some important foresight concepts and much more confident that you and your organization are asking the right questions.

And for those who dread picking up dry, academic treatises on a subject, have no fear. If the book's short length didn't already clue you in, be assured that we're not going to spend any time diving into the deeper philosophies or theories swirling around beneath the approaches presented here. For those interested in delving deeper into foresight, futures studies, and how these subjects integrate with planning, look through the additional resources at the end of this book and contact us for one of our training workshops.

Otherwise, this is all about getting straight to the action.

Who Should – and Who Shouldn't – Expect to Find Value in This Book

If you've been tasked with organizing the annual planning retreat or leading the new strategy effort or with reporting on the future of "x" to your leadership, then this book will be a valuable tool for quickly picking up some basics on how to think about the future and how to structure your organization's efforts at developing foresight. Likewise, if you now find yourself confronted with perhaps some deep and unsettling uncertainties about where your industry, business, or community is going, this book will give you a straight forward framework for structuring your thinking and for organizing discussions or projects.

What this book won't do is tell you how to "predict" the outcomes of this year's legislative session or accurately guess what will be the most popular color among your customers next year. The process and techniques in this book won't help you calculate the optimal budget allocations for next year and they won't help you estimate the probability of Company A being acquired by Company B in the next eighteen months. This book is not about divining the immediate or the hyper specific; this book is about how to explore the broader mid- to long-term futures in which your organization may soon find itself.

And if you're still with us at this point, go ahead and hit the next page!

Introduction

We all are interested in the question, "How is [*your thing*] going to change in the future?" Everyone has a natural instinct to be concerned about the future and virtually everyone at various points and in various ways tries to wrestle with the question, "what will the future bring?" Over the millennia, just about every culture on the planet has developed rituals and theories for divining or anticipating the future: oracles, throwing bones, watching the stars, etc... Many of these techniques were thought to be connected somehow with higher powers or deeper realities of the world, thus they could allow us to peek behind the curtain to glimpse what was to come.

Today we tend not to believe in such practices anymore but, living in a world of apparently rapid change, we are more concerned than ever with the future. Many of us intuitively sense that, increasingly, tomorrow will not be like yesterday. And while most of us don't read tea leaves or consult oracles before making important decisions, more and more of us are looking to develop *foresight* in

> "*...think of* foresight *simply as insight into how and why the future will be different from today.*"

order to gain a better understanding of what all is happening around us and how it might shape the future of our community, industry, or country.

how future will be diffred or could be

Let's think of foresight simply as *insight into how and why the future will be different from today*. In its modern form foresight is not, as any academically trained futurist will tell you, about *knowing* the future before it happens. That kind of knowledge, if it existed, would come from clairvoyance, something we most definitely don't address in this book. Instead, foresight is insight into what could be, not what will be. This distinction between insight into what's possible versus certitude over what precisely will happen is important enough that we will repeat it: foresight is insight into how the future could be different from today; it is not about the ability to see the future before it happens.

This might seem like some weird academic point to harp on, but we want to make sure that you don't end up confusing the model in this book with an exercise that tries to "get the future right." You won't be able to do that. In fact, no one can (their $5,000 money-back-guaranteed seminars notwithstanding). It is important to remember that the point of foresight is not to predict but to gain insight, insight that can both improve your current strategy and also help you rethink your basic goals and preferences for the future. And it is the creation of foresight that is at the heart of the *4 Steps to the Future* model.

The *4 Steps to the Future* Model
One of the things that the *4 Steps to the Future* model helps you with is context and "the bigger picture," so before we get to the model itself let's start by putting the model in its own context. The model presented in this book leads you through the first two

of three key steps in the larger cycle of foresight, planning, and action that all organizations (should) go through. Reduced to its simplest formulation, we try to develop foresight, which we use to inform our vision of the future we want to achieve, and then we develop strategy to make that future happen (see figure 1). And of course, as soon as we start implementing any strategy or plan, things start to happen, the world continues to change, other people react with their own plans, etc., all of which feeds back to us and requires us to develop some new foresight, rethink our goals, alter our strategies...

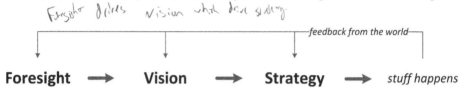

Figure 1: Larger Cycle of Foresight, Planning, and Action

The *4 Steps to the Future* model addresses the first two steps in figure 1, namely Foresight and Vision. It doesn't cover strategy formulation or execution, though those are also important areas to understand. In this book, we're just covering foresight and vision.

And just what is the model? The *4 Steps to the Future* model is quite simply:

1. Past
2. Present
3. Futures
4. Aspiration

It's that simple! Well, not really, of course, but we'll get to the details in just a bit. For now, let's consider why these are the four important steps in the model. First, we look at the Past because it helps us understand how we got to where we are and it often provides clues as to what might come next. Second, looking at the Present is all about taking stock of what is going on now and the signals we are receiving today about change. Third, Futures builds on the Past and the Present to take us into forecasting and exploring how the future might be different from today. Finally, Aspiration gets us back to the question of where we want to go and what we want to accomplish, using all of our thinking from Past, Present, and Futures as important inputs.

To "operationalize" this model, as they would say, we expand this outline of four steps to ask a set of basic but key questions. The sections that follow go into more detail for each step of the model, but for now we can quickly review the basic questions that allow us to fill in the model with answers and insights. The call out box shown here presents the key questions we explore in each step of the model.

The *4 Steps to the Future* model is not simply a list of questions, but is also a process with its own tools and worksheets to guide you and your group through the process. figure 2 on page 4 provides a flowchart of the *4 Steps* process.

The 4 Steps Model:

1. Past
   a. How has [your issue] changed over the last several years?
   b. Why did those changes happen?
2. Present
   a. Which of those forces are at work again?
   b. What new sources of change?
   c. What things will slow or prevent change?
3. Futures
   a. What are logical alternative futures for [your issue]?
   b. What are the opportunities and threats?
   c. Who will resist, channel, or accelerate change?
4. Aspiration
   a. What new goals?
   b. What new vision?

In later sections of the book we will expand upon each of these steps and look at the key questions we have to ask and learn about the tools we can use to help answer those questions. But, before we go, let's go over some important information.

Futures Studies

A great many professionals are engaged in trying to "predict" what will happen in the future. The concepts and tools presented in this book come from *futures studies*, which is a little-known and often misunderstood academic field that is mainly concerned with understanding and anticipating change in society. Graduates from futures studies are known as futurists, and they will all tell you that they do not predict the future; instead, they do a range of forecasting for clients. And as you'll see in this book, no where will you be advised on how to accurately predict a single future on which you should bet the entire organization's future.

We won't take up much space here talking about the field of futures studies. For those interested in finding out more about formal academic training in futures you will find a listing of some of the current programs out there in Additional Resources. For now, let's just consider three important principles of formal futures studies that are critical for getting the most value out of the *4 Steps* model.

Principles:
- The future does not exist (we're all helping to create it)
- There are many possible futures
- Those futures are constantly in flux

(handwritten margin note: Future doesn't exist, strategy ...)

We're not trying to get too deep here, but it is important to consider that, in fact, "the future" does not exist. It's not waiting patiently out there for us to catch up to it and it is not preordained or already written down in what would certainly have to be a very heavy book. And because it does not exist (yet) and because it isn't preprogrammed or set in stone, until the future happens, there are possibilities. And you, me, and everyone else reading this book each have a role to play in pushing us all towards or away from those possibilities. Thus, those "possible futures" are constantly shifting and changing based on the things we do, how we react, and how many other processes out there in the world (universe, really) unfold.

Keep these principles in mind and you will both arm yourself against those who try to sell you on their ability to predict the future and you will prevent yourself from ever thinking that there is nothing you or your organization can do to help shape a more desirable future.

The 4 Steps to the Future Process

The *4 Steps to the Future* model addresses the first two steps in the larger foresight and planning process that organizations follow.

Larger Cycle of Foresight, Planning, and Action

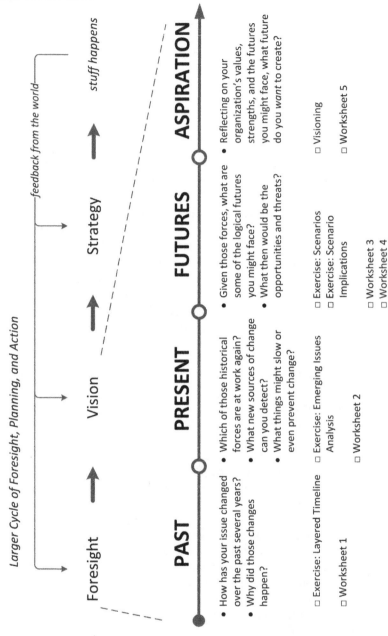

Figure 2: 4 Steps Overall Process

Everyday Practices and Ground Rules

While the previous list provided a set of overarching principles for doing futures work the following list is a short set of everyday practices that will serve you well as you work to produce real foresight with your organization. These are the types of things that academically trained futurists do all the time, every day, and are part of the reason why they can do what they do. These are only suggestions but we *really* encourage you to try them. Seriously, try 'em; you'll like 'em!

A. Expose yourself to lots of stuff: professional futurists usually do this through scanning, but many are also avid readers and love to constantly learn new subjects.

B. Break out of bounds: explore other sectors, industries, and regions; this will give you alternative and provocative perspectives from which to view and reframe your own industry or community.

C. Think (and take notes) visually: "visualization" is certainly all the rage right now, and for good reason: it helps tremendously with thinking through complex and interrelated issues.

D. Keep asking why?: the world is in fact a complex, densely interdependent set of systems... that means that we have to do a lot of probing into connections, causes, and our own assumptions.

E. Prompt others to consider what if?: we also need to keep everyone's minds (including our own) flexible by asking about not just what we expect to happen, but what logically could happen.

Now that we've covered both the underlying principles for futures and a few useful everyday habits for foresight professionals, let's look at the few important ground rules for actually using the *4 Steps* model. We're not saying that you won't succeed if you break these rules, but your project or process will produce much *better* outcomes if you and your fellow participants embrace these rules.

1. Stop trying to hit the bull's-eye: foresight is not for prediction

2. Keep numbers in their place: "hard" data are great for describing history, less so for describing a nonexistent future

3. Collect lots of stuff: we need to collect lots of signals of change: historical trend data, weak signals of emerging change, competing images of the future, etc.

4. Be ruthless with expectations: every time someone utters the phrase, "Yeah, but that won't happen," hit 'em with an, "And why?"

5.   Take everyone's input: all *perspectives* are valid and diversity of thought is important

6.   Do this every year: if foresight work is like the flu vaccine, then you need to routinely get boosters because that pesky little virus (the future) is constantly changing

7.   In fact, do a little bit of this all the time: if foresight work is like dental hygiene, then you'll want to brush and floss daily, otherwise that once a year check-up could be a doozy...

If this all seems like a lot to remember, then just copy out the Quick Reference sheet that we've included in the Appendices as a handy reference guide. You can also download a nice full size copy of it from www.visionforesightstrategy.com.

How This Book is Organized
This book is organized into four major sections, each corresponding to the four steps in the model: Past, Present, Futures, and Aspiration. Each section will be further divided into a brief description of the step, an introduction to a tool that you can use to help answer the critical questions, and an example of an organization that used the tool to explore its own futures.

We have included a fifth section of Additional Resources, which will provide you with more information about futures and foresight training as well as recommended reading for those wanting to dive deeper into some of the subjects addressed in this book.

But First, Before We Begin...
Before you jump into actually generating foresight with your organization, we need to take a moment to talk about your internal organizational context and some of the success factors we want to try to improve before you even begin organizing your foresight effort. Futures work, like any sort of planning or planning-related project, can only flourish in supportive environments. It is, in fact, a somewhat fragile species, and a harsh organizational environment will kill futures thinking or foresight work right on the vine. With that in mind, let's make sure that:

☐   Your organization is *not* in the midst of a the-house-is-burning-down crisis
☐   You have senior management support
☐   The effort has adequate time and resources
☐   Other planning and decision making processes within the organization are prepared to accept the foresight output (and that the foresight output is designed with them in mind)
☐   You have a good sense of the personalities and biases of the leadership and participants
☐   The project involves a decent cross section of the organization
☐   The project involves some outside perspective

If you can check off each one of those boxes, then you're in outstanding shape! Even if you're missing a couple of those boxes, then you're in pretty good shape to proceed. If, however, several of those boxes are unchecked, then it is well worth the time and effort to pause and work on changing conditions so that you can check everything off the list. And while it is beyond the scope of this book to provide specific guidance on these sorts of "pre-conditions," it is very important to consider these issues before launching (or even designing) a foresight process for your organization. For many of you, your foresight "process" might simply entail one half day of a company retreat, but for most organizations even half a day of the entire leadership team's attention is an extremely valuable resource that you'll want to use in the most productive way possible.

Past

Step number one in doing good foresight is – not surprisingly – to look backward. While the point of foresight is to develop insight into what *could* happen, trained futurists almost always begin their work by looking to the past to try to understand what *has* happened, what has not, and why. Developing a better understanding of the past doesn't tell us what will happen in the future, but it does give us an appreciation for the patterns that recur, the cycles that might be at work, and the roles that chance and randomness have played in creating our present. To paraphrase Mark Twain, history doesn't precisely repeat, but it does tend to rhyme. In order to do a better job anticipating the future we first have to talk about that tendency of history to rhyme.

In this first step of the *4 Steps to the Future* model, we're going to ask two basic questions: how has your issue/industry/community changed over the last several years, and why did those changes happen?

Question 1: How has [your thing] changed over the last 50 years?

Many of us spend a lot of time obsessing over how much the world is changing around us. Likewise, many of us effortlessly conjure images of how the future will be better or worse for us. What most of us don't do, however, is start by simply asking, "what actual changes have happened in the past, and why?" This is where we start our process, by looking backward to history to begin to understand the forces and factors that have shaped the world in which we now live.

Spending time looking back 15, 25, or even 50 years may seem like an academic exercise, but it has a number of clear and immediate benefits for our thinking about the future and for our group or organization. In terms of improving our thinking about the future, reviewing history helps to remind us of the important changes that have already occurred in our industry or community. It gives us the opportunity to connect the major milestones and headlines most of us recall with the underlying shifts and transformations that have periodically reshaped our issue. A historical review also reminds us that not every expected transformation actually came to pass; some things have remained largely unchanged over history. Reviewing what has changed, what has remained the same, and why helps us find the important patterns and relationships that drive or shape change.

For your group or organization, beyond the immediate work of producing foresight, the historical review exercise gives groups the opportunity to share important experiences and knowledge about the industry (or community) and about the organization itself. The historical review is for most groups a wonderful sharing and learning experience, giving everyone a better understanding of the organization and a better understanding of how the organization fits into the broader environment. Strengths, challenges, low points, high points; these are all recounted in compelling detail through the process of a historical review. Anyone participating in a historical review walks away with a better sense of not only *what* happened to the organization, but how it survived and continued to serve its mission and customers.

Question 2: Why did these changes happen?

Having explored how our issue has changed over the past 15, 25, or 50 years, we can turn to our second question, "*Why* did those changes occur?" Here we are asking about what *causes* change, not what specific changes happened. To avoid getting too deep into the intellectual weeds here, we will keep this very simple. In asking this question, we are trying to understand how much of history is the result of new science or technology, how much is driven by conflict or competition, how much is spurred by new ideas or values, and how much is simply unpredictable chance. Now, what do these mean?

- **Advancements in Science or Technology**: a lot of change has occurred in the last 250 years because of changes in our understanding of the physical world and the tools we create. Sir Isaac Newton's scientific discoveries, steam engines, electricity – all are examples of advances in science and technology that helped to drive significant change.

- **Conflict or Competition**: conflict between groups often drives change in society. Ideological contests between countries, domestic political struggles between elites and oppressed masses, competition between companies over customers and markets, and even "keeping up with the Joneses" are examples of competitive dynamics driving change.

- **New Ideas and Values**: change is also spurred by the introduction and spread of new ideas and philosophies (and these are often related to or in turn shape new technology or conflict). Faith in human rationality and science, the "Protestant work ethic," Marxist philosophy, and the popular myth of the college drop-out, geek programmer billionaire are all examples of new ideas and concepts instigating and shaping change.

- **Chance**: wild cards or emergent patterns of behavior that we cannot predict. Catastrophic natural disasters, meltdowns of nuclear power plants, assassinations, and stock market crashes are all examples of phenomena that we cannot exactly predict ahead of time, but which can prompt dramatic shifts in values and attitudes, in the structure of industries and communities, and in policy.

When reviewing the history of your issue, from which of these four categories has change been driven? Has one been dominant in driving change or has it come from a variety of areas? Can you see strong patterns in the history, or does it look fairly random over time? However the sources of change in your issue "bucket" into these four categories, we will call these the **Historical Drivers** of change for your issue. Many times in life the Historical Drivers are apparent in current changes we observe. While this is not always the case, it happens enough that we will draw upon these Historical Drivers again when we get to the Futures step later in the process.

So, now we can turn to the question of how you conduct a good historical review. For that we will use a tool called a Layered Timeline.

Tool for the Past: Layered Timeline

The layered timeline is an excellent tool for conducting a historical analysis, particularly for foresight work. Fundamentally, the layered timeline sees the world as divided into different levels, each of which experiences different types of change, which also tend to change at different rates. The top layer of the timeline is Daily Life where we are focused on the daily rhythms and experiences that individuals recognize. At the Daily Life layer we look at things like everyday practices and procedures, short-lived fads, rapidly spreading "memes" that flitter across the internet, and "politics." One layer down, at the Systems layer, we are looking at the longer-term structures of society: the institutions, rules, and even infrastructure that shape and constrain daily life. Here we talk about things like roads, major information technology systems, the structure of government agencies (their organization and relationships, not their daily politics), and laws and major policy positions. Finally, at the bottom-most layer we have Values. This layer is the deepest and is concerned with worldviews, deeply-held values, and the major "narratives" or stories that groups, communities, and societies use to interpret the world around them. At the Value level we look at things like the rise of "-isms" (e.g. environmentalism), dominant economic theories (e.g. Chicago school of economics), and the pursuit of work-life balance.

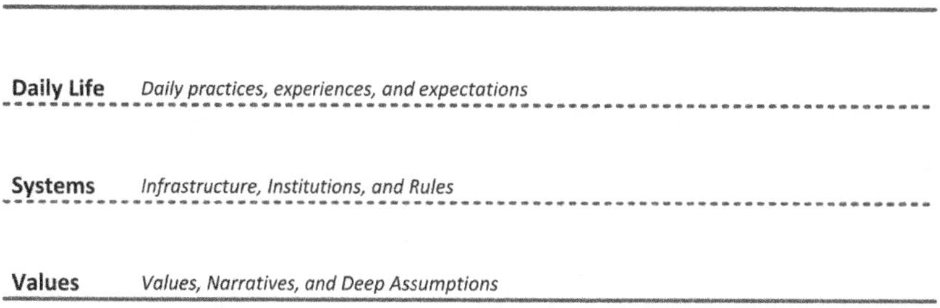

Figure 3: Layered Timeline

Generally speaking, things at the Daily Life layer change rapidly and much faster than those at the Systems layer, which in turn tend to change faster than things at the Values layer. Again, generally speaking, things at the Values layer take years, decades, or even generations to shift. At the Systems layer, things often take years to change, such as with organizational change. Things at the Daily Life layer tend to change in terms of days, weeks, and months. Not always true, but good as a general rule.

Main exercise

To conduct a historical analysis, you will use Worksheet 1 and the following process.

Step 1: you and/or group fill in the historical events above the timeline. These are the events and headlines that made the news and to which the history books refer. The passage of major pieces of legislation, wars, and pivotal moments of crisis or success are typically captured here.

Step 2: beyond the headlines of the past, what actually changed in your industry or community? Sometimes the events from above the timeline marked a change in direction, but other times they were just the end result of changes that had been underway for some time. Were people's purchasing habits changing? Were there important institutional changes underway? Had values been shifting or did they suddenly shift? Identify what actually changed and place these below the timeline.

Step 3: look at those changes you've identified, the ones below the timeline, and ask, "What caused those changes? In some cases, they may have been triggered by sudden, unexpected events that you captured above the timeline, but often change in industries and communities builds up or occurs because of larger forces or patterns that are at work. Identify what you think really caused those changes in terms of New Science and Technology, Conflict or Cooperation, New Ideas and Values, or unpredictable Chance.

Having trouble seeing the difference between Steps 1, 2, and 3, above? OK, let's look at an example:

Let's say we are concerned with the future of American security and foreign policy. We conduct a historical review, and in Step 1 we place a marker above the timeline in Worksheet 1 for "9/11." That was an *event* that occurred. But below the timeline, what changed or had been changing? For Step 2, *before* the 9/11 attack, we might put decades of conflicts and destabilization in places like Iraq, Iran, Afghanistan, and Pakistan, rising resentment against the United States among certain groups in the region, and the formation and evolution of certain terrorist organizations. After the attacks we might note sudden shifts in American values and priorities, major institutional shifts in military posture and structure, domestic policing and surveillance structure, and changes to daily life extending from TSA searches to overt and pervasive references to patriotism and American symbols in the media. Finally, for Step 3, we might place check marks in the boxes for Conflict and Competition and for New Ideas and Values and for Chance. Why? Because in terms of the *causes* of change in this instance, decades of American overt and covert intervention in the region (along with that of other powers such as the Soviet Union) were driven in part by Competition with the Soviets, spreading Islamic fundamentalism and anti-American sentiment, and the repurposing of anti-Soviet fighters into anti-American terrorists.

Bonus exercise: Finding connections between historical layers
For those of you who really enjoy the historical analysis exercise, you can tack on an additional exercise that will add another dimension to your analysis of history. The astute reader will note that the three layers in our layered timeline are all actually interrelated. Thus, one of the things futurists often do is to look for the connections between changes across those layers. In life, changes on one layer almost always ripple and have impacts on things at other layers. As a bonus exercise, look for what some of these connections may have been in the past and draw them onto the worksheet. These connections often reveal important systemic factors that play significant roles in shaping, channeling, or dampening change.

Historical Analysis in Action: Preparing for the Futures of Higher Education

The futures of formal education are an oft-talked about but difficult to forecast topic. In the course of our work with local communities we were introduced to a community college that was preparing for a new round of strategic planning. Well aware of the turbulent and uncertain changes underway in education, the chancellor of the college approached us about the possibility of doing some of the foresight work they had witnessed us doing with the community. Together we determined that a scenario project would be an excellent choice for the college as a springboard for strategic planning.

Over the course of three months, we worked with the college on developing an original set of scenario forecasts, using the focal issue of, "What roles might higher education play in the future of the community?" The project was built around two major workshops, the first of which focused on developing the basic scenarios and which started off with a historical timeline exercise. In this exercise the participants, which included faculty, staff, and key community stakeholders, discussed the emergence and evolution of community college education in the United States since its beginnings. The group plotted the major developmental milestones and turning points, debated the major external events occurring around those times in American history, and identified different eras in the evolution of community college education.

The historical analysis exercise was a key step in the project, one that not only surfaced important ideas incorporated into the later scenario forecasts, but one that also brought the participant group closer together. As a tool for foresight, it enabled the group to find important patterns in the history of community college education, which we later used to frame some of the subsequent scenario work. As a group experience, it served to enhance the overall, collective understanding of the roots of their college and the challenges and successes it had experienced throughout its history. The exercise was an important orienting step that got the entire, diverse group onto the same page and referencing the same shared history.

Now, let's take a quick breather while we use the image below to see where we are in the 4 Steps process and the kinds of thinking and the exercises we've gone over so far.

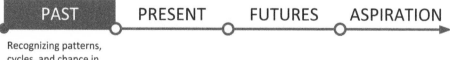

PAST   PRESENT   FUTURES   ASPIRATION

Recognizing patterns,
cycles, and chance in
your history.

☐ Layered Timeline

HISTORICAL ANALYSIS

This is the first of five worksheets in the 4 Steps model. What happened in the past? What drove change?

① **What Happened?**

What were the noteworthy events and headlines in this history?

50 years ago   25 years ago

② **What Changed?**

DAILY LIFE

Daily practices, experiences, and expectations

SYSTEMS

Infrastructure, Institutions, and Rules

VALUES

Values, Narratives, and Deep Assumptions

* Devar Fonddin
* Myanmar

4 Steps to the Future Worksheet 1

5 years ago

(3) **Why Did Those Changes Happen?**

☐ New Science and Tech

☐ Conflict & Competition

☐ New Ideas and Values

☐ Chance

☐ Other

We'll call these causes our **Historical Drivers** of change.

STEP 1: PAST

Present

The second step in the *4 Steps* model is the Present, and while the "present" is really just a transitory moment between what was and what might be, for our purposes the Present is where we take a look at all of the "signals" about change that we *presently* think we are receiving.

When it comes to signals about change, we are going to ask three things:

- Which of our Historical Drivers may be at work again today?

- What *new* sources of change do you think you are detecting?

- What things might slow or even prevent change today?

Your answers to these questions will form three buckets of building blocks that we will use later in Step 3, the Futures. For now, we just want to answer the questions and identify these futures building blocks.

Question 1: Which of the Historical Drivers are at work again?

In Step 1 you conducted a historical analysis to see what changed in history, what did not, and why. These we called the Historical Drivers. But now we want to see if any of those same forces are still at work driving and shaping change today. Which of your Historical Drivers – if any – seem to be at work again today driving change in your issue?

Question 2: What *New Sources* of change can you detect?

Beyond the historical patterns of change you identified during your historical analysis, what are some *new* sources of change that you can identify? Here we are talking about both *trends* and *emerging issues*, two concepts that can be related but which we will treat as two distinct things.

Trends

Put simply, a trend is a historical change over time. Trends are things for which we have some sort of quantitative data, from which we produce the trend lines of graphs. Trends are not the future. They are not even statements about the future. We often confuse a trend with a future state because, especially when we're looking at trend graphs, trend lines powerfully *imply* what the future will look like *if the trend lines don't change*. But it is important to remember that trends are merely descriptions about past change; there are normally a great many factors that will go into determining where that trend line will go in the years to come.

Having said that, trends are critically important building blocks for foresight, as they describe change that *has been* happening, calling our attention to important systemic issues and indicating from where some of the pressures for change have been coming. Examples of trends include the rising price of oil (or falling, depending on when you're reading this!), the growth in mobile phone subscriptions, and the rise in "meaningful use" of electronic medical records by physicians.

It is also important to keep in mind that when we identify trends we need to be clear about what the trend is and the direction of the trend. Often in workshops, when we ask participants to identify trends, some will throw out statements like, "the economy" or "oil." Neither of those examples describes actual trends. Better would be, "falling GDP growth rate" or "rising price of oil." Be as specific as possible and be clear about the direction of the trend.

Emerging Issues

Now, in contrast to trends, when we are talking about emerging issues we are talking about "weak signals" of change, where we are only just detecting something that *might* drive change in the future. Whereas trends have clear historical data that defines important factors or issues, emerging issues are suggestions for what might become important factors or issues. Thus, most of the things we identify here are not yet mainstream or mature, things like emerging technologies, future public policy issues, or new concepts, ideas, or philosophies that might be spreading.

Another way to see this is depicted in the s-curve graph in figure 4. Futurists use this to plot the emergence of new issues: the Foresight Zone (where futurists really like to live!) is where ideas and new technologies really exist at the fringes; those things that survive and continue to mature move into the Innovation Zone where things change more quickly and more people are joining the conversation or investing money; those things that survive that now start to become mainstream as they enter the Reactive Zone, so-called because at this stage if you're just hearing about this thing, your only option is to react to its existence; and finally a few things pass into The New Normal, becoming part of the unquestioned way to think and do things.

The bottom line with emerging issues is that they not be mainstream technologies or ideas; if what we're looking at is being debated down at the State legislature, then it is no longer an emerging issue. You want to be discussing things that are in the Foresight or Innovation Zones. A warning sign for you will be if your organization only wants to argue about things that fall in the Reactive Zone (or, heaven forfend, The New Normal!).

To help with identifying emerging issues, you can use the following three basic categories:

- **New Technologies**: guessing about how a new app, gadget, or technology is going to revolutionize the world has almost become a national past time in places like the United States. Yet, technology has been a central and increasingly dominant driver of social change in the world since the late 18th century. Here we're looking for not-yet-mature technologies that might have a significant impact on the future of our issue. A good example of what was an early stage emerging technology in the 1990s was rapid prototyping, which now goes by the label, "3D printing." This technology is much closer to the top

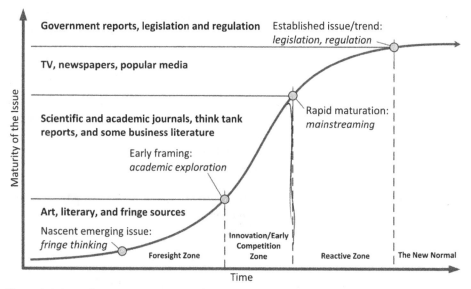

Figure 4: S-Curve for Emerging Issues Analysis

of the s-curve (see figure 4) and is expected to be mainstream in a mass retail sense in just a few years.

- **Potential Policy Issues**: another category we want to look for is things that might be important policy issues in the future. Here we are trying to identify future problems or issues long before they develop into full-blown public or legislative debates. A good example would be the aging of the Baby Boomers in the United States. In the 1980s, anyone doing simple demographic projections would have seen that in the future (today), there would be an unprecedented number of older citizens. A little foresight would have suggested that this generation would be more assertive and active than previous generations, and even simple analyses would have called attention to the healthcare and social welfare implications of so many more people retiring and needing services. In the 1980s this would have been an *emerging* issue. Today it is the stuff of debates, scrambling, and responding to imminent challenges. Additional examples would include gay marriage, legalization of marijuana, and net neutrality.

- **New Ideas or Concepts**: the third category we want to look for has to do with new concepts or thinking that is emerging somewhere in society and which might grow into an influential or disruptive viewpoint in the future. Again, we want to identify these earlier in their development rather than later, which gives us not only more time to react or prepare but, ideally, an opportunity to *shape* its future development. With new ideas, concepts, or philosophies, they often first emerge on the fringes, where outsiders, mavericks, or counter-culture types tend to speak. As they develop, these ideas continue to get refined and tested and tend to move up through academic writing and then into popular publications and finally into mainstream consciousness. Examples of new concepts which developed and diffused out into society include environmentalism, sustainability, design thinking, and "disruptive innovation."

It should go without saying at this point that there are often linkages between these three categories of emerging "stuff." Emerging technologies often suggest future policy issues (information technology and privacy), potential policy issues can provoke deep thinking that leads to new ideas or concepts (technology-driven unemployment prompting new ideas about "guaranteed basic income"), and new ideas can alter our interests or preferences for new technologies (interest in sustainability driving research into new energy and building technologies).

To further help your search for signals of emerging change, we're going to introduce two frameworks: a simple one and a more nuanced one. Both will help you to organize your thinking and your research. And we know which one you're going to pick... ☺

The Simple Framework: STEEP
The acronym STEEP stands for Social, Technological, Economic, Environmental, and Political, and it is a very common framework used by professional futurists for scanning and emerging issues analysis (more on this later). There have been many minor variations on STEEP around the world (PEST, SLEPT, PESTLE, etc...), but the basic framework is very helpful for ensuring that researchers have looked *broadly* at the environment in order to detect potential change. Essentially, STEEP asks you to look for signals of change within each one of these broad categories. No strange magic here, just straight forward broad thinking. Table 1 below would be a simple way of combining the previous three categories with the STEEP framework. Don't worry too much about duplication or getting things in the right boxes; the important point is to flush out a wide variety of emerging change.

Table 1: STEEP Framework

	Emerging Technology	Potential Policy Issues	New Ideas or Concepts
Social			
Technological			
Economic			
Environmental			
Political			

The More Nuanced Framework: Verge
For those interested in a framework that probes a little deeper into the nature of how our communities and industries are changing, the Verge General Practice Framework will be a useful tool. Verge was specifically developed as an alternative to the classic STEEP framework and took a different approach to the categories it uses to think about the broader environment. The Verge framework poses questions about six related aspects of life: how we define things; how we relate to one another; how we connect to

Table 2: Verge Framework

	Emerging Technology	Potential Policy Issues	New Ideas or Concepts
Define			
Relate			
Connect			
Create			
Consume			
Destroy			

one another; how we create value; how we consume value; and how we destroy value. Each of the six Verge domains is further defined below:

- *Define*: the Define domain speaks to the concepts, ideas, and paradigms we use to define ourselves and the world around us. This includes things like worldview, paradigms, and social values and attitudes.

- *Relate*: deals with the social structures and relationships that organize people and create organizations. Here we look at things like family structures, business models, and governance structures.

- *Connect*: encompasses the technologies and practices used to connect people, places, and things. Connect looks for things like information technology, urban design, and language.

- *Create*: concerned with the technology and processes through which we produce goods and services. This is all about things like manufacturing, efficiency, and rule-making.

- *Consume*: about the ways in which we acquire and use the goods and services we create. This domain is about issues like modes of exchange, consumer preferences, and marketing.

- *Destroy*: about the ways in which we destroy value and the reasons for doing so. Here we are concerned with phenomena like violence and killing, waste, and attempts to undermine rules and norms.

As with the STEEP framework, we can build a simple matrix to combine the original three categories with the Verge domains. For more on the Verge General Practice Framework, see Additional Resources.

Taken together trends and emerging issues form what we will call the **New Sources of Change**.

Now just to recap at this point, so far you should have a list of Historical Drivers and a list of New Sources of change. Reviewing things up to this point, we have:

- Question 1: Which of the historical drivers are at work again?
- Question 2: What *new sources* of change can you detect?
  - ○ Trends
  - ○ Emerging Issues
    - ▪ Three basic categories:
      - New technologies
      - Potential policy issues
      - New ideas or concepts
    - ▪ Frameworks for scanning
      - STEEP
      - Verge GPF

Next we will turn to some things that form counterpoints to the Historical Drivers and New Sources of change.

Question 3: What things might slow or prevent change?

Futurists are by nature and training fascinated by change in the world around them. Yet, at any given time, continuity from one day to the next is the most likely situation. Why? Because while change is indeed the one constant in the universe, there are still many forces that act to hold things steady, to keep things in place. This is particularly true for society, where we humans prefer a good dose of regularity in our daily affairs. In addition, changes or trends often provoke reactions and counter trends. And so, whenever we are doing foresight work we want to specifically look for those things that might either prevent some possible future from happening outright, or which might at least dampen the possible changes.

Common types of stability-enforcing things include:

- **Rules, customs, and traditions**: some of the most straightforward forces for continuity and stability (versus change) come from society itself in the form of laws and social conventions. In communities and institutions, it can be very hard to overcome "the way we do things", and existing rules and practices often prevent or even forbid the types of changes we can imagine.

- **Physical or logistical constraints**: physical realities also play a big role in dampening or preventing changes. Changes often require boring-sounding things like infrastructure, technical standards, and interoperability with existing systems, maintenance networks, and upstream and downstream services in a functioning supply chain... There are many pragmatic reasons why possible changes don't happen as fast as you expect, as dramatically as you expect, or simply fail to get off the ground.

- **Patterns of behavior**: another source of stability comes from the well-known tendency of humans to be creatures of habit. As psychologists like to point out, the best predictor of future behavior is past behavior, and this often (though never always) holds for individuals as well as for larger groups of humans. As much as many of us *say* we want change, we often seek out and reinforce old patterns and processes.

- **Powerful stakeholders or incumbents**: a final source of resistance to change very often comes from powerful stakeholders in your community or industry. People often don't like change, particularly so for leaders and organizations that currently benefit the most from the way things exist today. When those in organizations or in markets detect new challenges to the status quo (change), they typically react to prevent or dampen that change. Industry groups will put pressure on lawmakers to prevent disruption to their industry, businesses will move to block, imitate, or buy up new competitors, and community groups will organize to block new development.

We will call these various anti-change forces **Stabilities**, and we will use them along with Historical Drivers and New Sources of change in Step 3, Futures.

Note: the point in looking for forces that will stop or dampen change is not to argue for why the world won't change (because, trust us, it will), but rather to inject just a bit of sober thinking to help make our forecasting more realistic and thus, more valuable. Resistance to change is something we see every day and it plays an important role in shaping the pathways that events follow and thus, the futures we end up living.

Tool for the Present: Emerging Issues Analysis

While just about every profession involved in looking towards the future uses trends in some fashion, one of the practices that distinguishes professional futurists is something called *emerging issues analysis* (EIA). Put simply, it's the practice of identifying those emerging issues we just discussed. To keep things simple, we'll say that EIA has two steps: 1) scan lots and lots of information, in order to; 2) detect patterns and weak signals of change.

Step 1 is often referred to as "scanning," and when we say that you look over a lot of information, we're not kidding. This isn't research in the typical sense where someone digs deep for a lot of specific information about one thing; this is about quickly scanning a very broad array of information sources, without necessarily diving into too much detail initially. Once you do start to detect some patterns or what might be definitive signals of change, then you switch modes – so to speak – and begin to focus in and clarify what you might be detecting.

And this isn't rocket science: it's about scanning the world around you for *lots* of signals, sifting and sorting all of those signals, and selecting out certain things. And if all else fails, go back to the s-curve chart on page 18: you want to find things that fit into the Foresight and Innovation Zones. If your "emerging issues" are all logically situated towards the top of the s-curve, then you're not looking at the right things!

Main exercise

For this exercise you're going to be using one tool (EIA) and one of the two frameworks introduced earlier (either STEEP or Verge). Oh, and you're going to use Worksheet 2, so be sure to print that and lay it out in front of you.

Step 1: identify the major trends that are driving change in your business, industry, or community. Don't forget to be as specific as possible and to clearly identify the direction of change. It's not necessarily critical here, but Worksheet 2 asks you to separate increasing from decreasing trends, mostly just to make sure you think of both types of trends. Refer back to whichever of the two frameworks (STEEP or Verge) you chose to use. Did you cast a wide enough net?

Step 2: now see if you can legitimately identify counter trends that are rising in reaction to the trends you just identified. These are of course trends in their own right, but they can play a critical role in deflecting, slowing, or stopping change from altering the status quo.

Step 3: using the s-curve chart and the framework you chose (STEEP or Verge), identify a wide variety of emerging issues. Whereas with trends you may have only identified a handful that are important, with emerging issues we want you to identify as many as is practicable. Rule of thumb: have at least 3 times as many emerging issues as you do trends. Don't worry too much at this point about how crazy they might seem; remember that most things far down on the s-curve and deep in the Foresight Zone are most likely to sound crazy because they are specifically about the potential for change away from the status quo. Finally, for each of your emerging issues, make a simple forecast: when will that issue "top" the s-curve?

Step 4: now we move away from the New Sources of change (trends and emerging issues) and make a quick stop to look for Stabilities, those additional things that will slow or prevent change. Using the basic categories explained earlier and shown on Worksheet 2, try to identify the real forces that support the status quo.

Emerging Issues Analysis in Action: Scanning for Emerging Change with a Fortune 50 Company

Organizations with global operations face a particular level of complexity and uncertainty when it comes to contemplating "the future," and often require approaches to framing and exploring their futures that are both nuanced and rigorous. It was in this context that a major global food and beverage company established a large initiative to explore a range of foresight methods. As part of the team brought in to help guide these efforts we had the opportunity to work with the company's long range research divisions as they worked through an integrated sequence of foresight projects. And as one would expect, one of the opening projects was a series of horizon scans to identify relevant trends and emerging issues that would be used later as input to scenario development.

The overall flow of the initiative started with scanning and emerging issues analysis, which then proceeded to scenario development, and then on to research portfolios. As is the wont of large corporations with sizable budgets, the client commissioned horizon scans from three different foresight consultants, producing a veritable avalanche of rich information about potential changes in the global landscape. These companies applied different scanning frameworks to identify important trends, counter trends, and potential emerging issues across a wide array of areas and looking out over the next couple of decades. Our team's work began with collecting this information, along with a detailed inventory of other existing internal foresight material, and augmented by live presentations by respected external experts, and guiding the client through "sense-making" with the resulting mass of information. This we did through workshops with different groups of internal researchers, scientists, and managers, using futures research methods to reframe the material and explore its implications for the future.

This horizon scanning and emerging issues analysis was a critical component in the long term success of the project. Such a rich mass of information about changes in the external environment – and about changes both on the horizon and further over the horizon – could not help but push participants out beyond their comfort zones to explore changes in technologies and business opportunities they had scarcely heard of before. The workshops gave participants the structure to analyze the content and to identify important issues that went on to critically define the subsequent scenario work (discussed in a later section). This step in the process also provided employees with an opportunity to see patterns and disconnects between the time when certain technologies would come online versus when the company would be positioned to take advantage of them. On more than one occasion, the emerging issues material featured in the workshops confronted participants with challenging questions about the long-term viability and social acceptability of certain traditional lines of business.

Now, let's take a quick breather while we use the image below to see where we are in the 4 Steps process and the kinds of thinking and the exercises we've gone over so far.

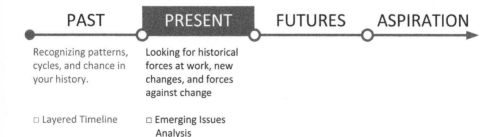

PAST	PRESENT	FUTURES	ASPIRATION
Recognizing patterns, cycles, and chance in your history.	Looking for historical forces at work, new changes, and forces against change		
□ Layered Timeline	□ Emerging Issues Analysis		

TRENDS, EMERGING ISSUES, AND STAB

Together our Trends and Emerging issues are what
we'll call our **New Drivers** of change.

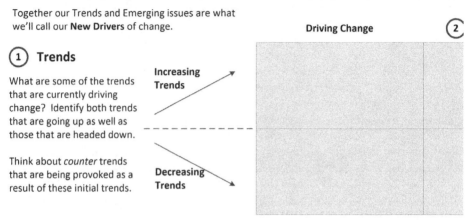

① Trends

What are some of the trends
that are currently driving
change? Identify both trends
that are going up as well as
those that are headed down.

Think about *counter* trends
that are being provoked as a
result of these initial trends.

③ Emerging Issues

What new ideas, issues, or technologies are below the radar
now, but might mature into important drivers of change?

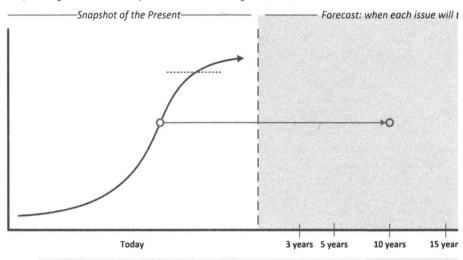

ILITIES

) **Counter Trends**

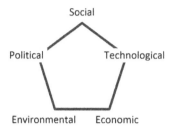

The STEEP framework.

(4) **Stabilities**

What things will slow or prevent change? We'll call these our **Stabilities**.

Common types of stability-enforcing things:

- Rules, customs, and traditions
- Physical or logistical constraints
- Patterns of behavior
- Powerful stakeholders or incumbents

s   20 years   25 years

STEP 2: PRESENT

Futures

The third step in the *4 Steps* model is to take the Historical Drivers, the New Sources of change, and the Stabilities you identified in the first two steps (the Past and the Present) and use them as building blocks to forecast alternative possible futures. In essence, the Futures step asks one deceptively simple question, "What are the possible futures of [your issue]?"

To be fair, depending on the timeframe you use, the number of different possible futures for your issue could be quite large. The farther out in time we look the exponentially greater the number of possible futures (see figure 5). Unfortunately, you probably have neither the resources nor the time to try to comprehensively explore all of those possibilities. No, like all of us, you need a practical way to cut through the uncertainty and do some good thinking about the future. And the way that the Futures step will help you do that is through developing *scenarios*.

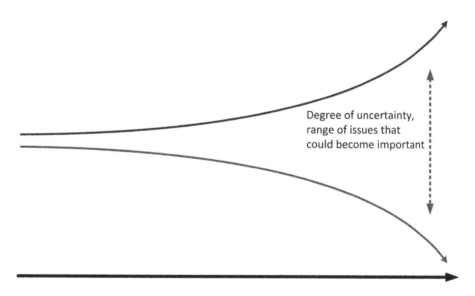

Degree of uncertainty, range of issues that could become important

Figure 5: Cone of Uncertainty/Range of Futures

Change and Disruption

Before we get into the fun of developing scenarios (and it *is* fun!), we need to make a quick pit stop to load up on a simple framework that we will use when we do forecast scenarios. Thus we want to briefly consider the different types of change we observe in the world and we want to look at something called the disruption pyramid.

Types of Change
The issue of change is at the heart of both futures studies and foresight. There are many different typologies of change – different ways to categorize the types of change we see in life. The *4 Steps* model uses a simple but useful typology that distinguishes between *continuity*, *incremental change*, and *abrupt change*. Scholars could get into long, boring debates about what fits into these categories and why each one occurs, but again we're going to keep things simple.

- *Continuity*: things stay the same. The way we do things and why we do them that way remain fundamentally unchanged. Oh yes, this season's color might be pink rather than black and every electronics manufacturer might be touting their new "revolutionary" product, but the important structures and relationships in life stay the same.

- *Incremental Change*: important patterns in life are in fact changing, just not very quickly. Think about how large organizations do in fact change, it's just that they can take a while to do it. This is often the result of many people chipping away at old ways of doing things as everyone tries to adapt to the external environment.

- *Abrupt Change*: for most futurists this is the sexy stuff! This is the sudden ecosystem collapse, the quick merger of two companies, or the popular rebellion that overthrows an authoritarian regime. All are examples of a system jumping from one state to another. Abrupt change is dramatic and almost always involves turbulence and disruption.

When it comes to most institutions in society, on a day to day basis, continuity is really the most likely outcome. Where there is change to be observed, it's typically of the incremental variety. Least likely is the sexy and disruptive abrupt change. Yet, because of its material and emotional impact, we do in fact spend a lot of time trying to understand, anticipate, and in some cases trigger abrupt change.

These categories are important for our purposes because the *4 Steps* model uses them to frame four basic scenario arcs, which you will use as the "backbones" for forecasting alternative futures.

Disruption Pyramid
Another simple framework that we incorporate into the *4 Steps* model is our disruption pyramid, which focuses attention on the type of disruption that your organization will encounter in any given scenario. The pyramid, which is shown in figure 6 below, looks at five different scales of disruption, from a society-wide change in the underlying paradigm to a very surface-level and minimally disruptive change (relatively speaking) to products and services. Things at the top of the pyramid happen more often but have less wide-ranging impacts while things towards the bottom happen less often but impart more dramatic changes.

Figure 6: Disruption Pyramid

The point to the pyramid, which will be used after your scenarios are developed, is to provide a way to categorize – and to compare – the type of disruption and changes your organization will face across the different scenarios you forecast. It also provides a nice way to double check that the specific implications you identify from each scenario are in alignment with the overall impact of the scenario.

And now, on to the main event!

Scenarios: Many Possible Futures
Put simply, scenarios are descriptions of alternative possible futures. Scenarios are one of the workhorse tools in futures studies, playing a central role both in anticipating possible change and in generating visions of preferred futures. Scenarios are a mainstay tool for us because they allow us to: a) deal with uncertainty and limited information by forecasting *multiple* scenarios at a time; b) explore and convey complex situations and changes in an easy-to-understand format, and; c) provide groups with compelling images of counter-intuitive or unconsidered possibilities about the future.

Scenarios were popularized by the Global Business Network (GBN) in the 1990s, which used a particular approach to developing and using scenarios that they called "scenario planning." GBN-style scenario planning is recognizable by its characteristic 2x2 matrix (see figure 7, below). To be clear, there are *many* methods for producing scenarios. In the *4 Steps* model we're going to show you one method that is both easy to grasp and provides more structure than the common 2x2 method, with the added benefit of ensuring that you produce a realistic yet challenging range of future possibilities.

It is critically important to emphasize that scenarios are not predictions. Indeed, how could they be when there are typically 3, 4, 5, or even 6 scenarios all covering the same future time period? No, scenarios are at most *forecasts* of logical but different ways in which the future could unfold. Once again, scenarios are not attempts to get the future "right" but rather structured ways of exploring possible futures.

This point – that you are not trying to get the future right by identifying the single one that will come to pass – is important enough that we'll try to drive the point home with a bit of an analogy. In marksmanship the idea is to hit the bull's-eye, over time demon-

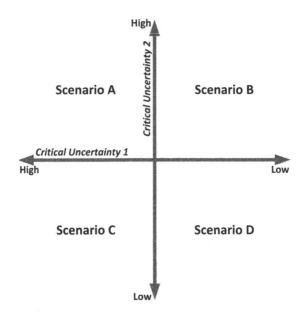

Figure 7: Generic 2x2 Scenario Matrix

strating both precision and accuracy. Now, the beginner, who may have never handled a rifle before, will tense their entire body and often hold their breath in an effort to hold the rifle as still as possible. Intuitive, but wrong. The marksman learns of the need to relax. They learn that once your body is as still as possible in a good, supported position (not using your trembling muscles to hold everything in place), there remains your natural "wobble," because – you know – your heart is still beating. And they learn that the round firing should be almost a surprise, so relaxed are they in the process of shooting.

Now let's contrast marksmanship with the art of forecasting futures. Like in marksmanship, when most people come to the work of forecasting the future their intuition tells them they should intellectually *squeeze* to hold everything still in their effort to "hit" the bull's-eye. This takes the form of more data, more modeling, and more everything, all in an attempt to get that rifle steadier and steadier in order to hit that target, precisely and accurately. But the problem is that the target they are trying to hit – "the future" – *doesn't exist*. Unlike in marksmanship, where there really is a small little dot out there on a sheet of paper, in foresight work there is no actual target, nothing to actually study and range. No amount of data or computational power will ever reduce your forecasting wobble to zero because the universe hasn't produced your "target" yet.

Don't forget: you, me, your coworkers and family, and strangers on the other side of the planet are all right now creating the future through our actions and interactions, coupled with the myriad natural processes occurring everywhere right now. In one sense, the future doesn't exist because we all haven't yet created it. And keep in mind that we all have less influence shaping tomorrow (i.e. the day after today) than we do next year, over which we have less influence than some time five years from today.

> "...the metric of success for scenario work is not whether or not you got the future "right"; it's whether or not they inspired and informed action that, years later, you are happy to have taken."

So, whereas in marksmanship you are trying to reduce the size of your shot group (the circle in which all of your shots fall) and get it consistently onto the bull's-eye, in foresight work you are trying to do the *opposite*. You're not trying to hit what does not yet exist (a single point in the future); you're trying to expand your shot group to give yourself a better picture of the boundaries of what's logically possible in the future. And why, again? Because the future is not a single inevitable outcome; it is always a *range of possible outcomes*. And the farther into the future you're trying to think, the wider you need to make that shot group, because the greater the range of possible futures.

This is part of the reason why scenarios have become such a mainstay in futures and foresight work: they inherently capture the uncertainty and multiplicity that characterizes the future.

We should note here that in generating scenarios you do, in fact, want data and models and whatnot; you just aren't using them with the expectation of getting close to identify the one "right" future, the bull's-eye. Rather, you're using things like trend data and good theory to model realistic and likely types of actions, interactions, and outcomes so that your scenarios – for as divergent as you want them to be – are grounded in observable human and social patterns of behavior.

We also need to note here that in developing scenarios you're not trying make "good" or "bad" scenarios. The exercise isn't about spinning fabulous fantasies or painting serious doom and gloom; it is about telling *logical* stories about how things might change. A good rule of thumb here is that each scenario you forecast should have elements that some readers will consider positive and some elements they will consider negative. No future is entirely awesome or horrible and neither should your scenarios be either good or bad.

Ultimately, the metric of success for scenario work is not whether or not you got the future "right"; it's whether or not they inspired and informed action that, years later, you are happy to have taken.

The Focal Issue
Forecasting scenarios is aided hugely by having what folks in the trade call a "focal issue." This is the question about the future that you want to ask, the thing you really want to explore. And as the name implies, this is about *focus*. So, instead of simply asking, "What's the future of education?" state education leaders might ask, "how might online learning and alternative credentialing reshape learning pathways." But this is art rather than science, and the precise focus depends entirely upon the group conducting the scenario work and the world as they perceive it.

A good way to approach developing the focal issue is to think about scope and timeframe. Scope is concerned with both the scale of your question (say, local, national, or global) and the specificity (e.g. "the economy" vs. workforce development). It is important to get scope right: too broad of a scope and the issue is too big and unwieldy and the scenarios will necessarily have to be less deep into the topic; too narrow and you will fail to account for enough of the connections and influences from developments in the broader environment. Timeframe is pretty straightforward, but again you want to think a bit before deciding on the time horizon for the scenarios. Too close to the present (say, 18 months) and there may not be enough time for important shifts and changes to occur, yet too far (say, 50 years from now) and most of the forecast could be irrelevant for the decision making you are trying to inform.

Table 3: Examples of Focal Issues

Less useful	More useful
"What's the future of the economy?"	"How will digital fabrication impact business models over the next 20 years?"
"What's the future of banking?"	"How will disruptive technologies impact retail banking by 2030?"
"How will the School Board change policies in the next two years?"	"How will state education transform itself in the next decade?"

As soon as you've crafted your perfect focal issue you can move onto actually generating scenarios.

Scenario Types

The *4 Steps* model provides you with four basic scenarios to build, each defined in terms of change. Hopefully you recall the earlier discussion of different types of change (if not, stop now and jump back to that discussion earlier in this section of the book), because the four scenario types are based on variations of those basic types of change: continuity, incremental, and abrupt. The table below lays out the scenario types and the characteristics of each.

Table 4: Scenario Types

Type	Scenario Characteristics
Type A	Continuity (more of the same)
Type B	Incremental change, low level of disruption
Type C	Incremental change, high level of disruption
Type D	Abrupt change

Type A represents what we generally expect, at least unconsciously, of the future: that life will continue basically as we've known it. The challenge with this type of scenario is in justifying why, in the face of all of the push for change you identified in the Historical Drivers and New Sources of change, nothing meaningful happens. That might sound easy, but it can be challenging to logically and reasonably counter *every* trend or force for change. Type B scenarios have change occurring, but the nature of the change, either in scale, scope, or just timing, means that people experience relatively mild disruption to core relationships and practices. Referencing the Disruption Pyramid from earlier, Type B scenarios tend to occur at the upper levels of the pyramid. Type C scenarios also see incremental change, but in these cases the disruptions occur lower on the Disruption Pyramid. Finally, Type D scenarios introduce relatively sudden and certainly dramatic changes. As in Type A scenarios, these might seem easy to forecast, but here the challenge is reversed: finding the logical pathways that lead us from the present to a dramatically changed future often require us to expose and challenge core assumptions about why the world works the way it currently does.

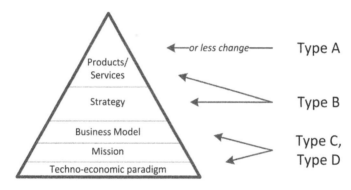

Figure 8: Disruption Pyramid with Scenario Types

The way we use these scenario types, which will be explained in greater detail in the Main Exercise below, is that we ask, what combination of Historical Drivers, New Sources of change, and Stabilities combine to produce these different types of scenarios? In this way the scenario types are the patterns and the Drivers, Sources, and Stabilities you identified earlier become the building blocks. Using patterns based on how things change, and using unique combinations of the scenario building blocks specific to the history and the present of your particular issue, you will construct four different but logical possible futures for your issue.

Scenario Implications: So, What Does This All Mean?
When you hang out with professional futurists, you'll probably hear them mention that it is the *process* of scenario building, the experience of creating them that imparts the greatest value for those who participate in the process. We would echo that sentiment. But the experience and the process is of course not the only point of value creation. Scenarios are used quite explicitly to do things like test strategy, explore contingencies, and spur creativity and innovation. In this sub section we will look at a few of the ways in which groups explore the *implications* of scenarios.

Stakeholders, Old and New
One of the great discussions to have is what you might call "futures stakeholders analysis," in which you use the scenarios to help identify current and future potential stakeholders, how each would react to the scenarios, and the actions they would likely take as a result. To do this we use a simple framework built around the three basic reactions that individuals and groups have to the possibility of change: resisting change, channeling change, and accelerating change.

Resisters: these are the groups and/or key individuals who essentially have a conservative view (in the generic, not American political sense) of your issue; these groups like or prefer the status quo and thus resist the possibility of change; they may even deny the possibility of change

Channelers: these are groups that recognize that change is inevitable and accept that fact; they work to channel the changes they observe as best as possible to align with their values and preferences

Accelerators: these are the stakeholders who essentially have a radical view, meaning that they want more change around your issue; in essence they want to "put the pedal to the metal" on change; for these groups more change is better, and often the more the better

Possible stakeholder groups include: customers, vendors and suppliers, partners, competitors, regulators, community members, and shareholders.

Because the scenarios are descriptions of possible futures, we not only need to ask how the current stakeholders would react to the emergence of each scenario, we also need to ask what new stakeholders might emerge *because* of the scenario? This might be less likely in scenario Types A and B – though still a possibility that needs to be considered – but it becomes much more likely as you consider the significant changes that occur in Types C and D.

And while it is easier to identify possible new stakeholders in more disruptive scenarios like Types C and D, all of the scenarios are describing systems of people, structures, and nature, which mean that there are always complex dynamics at play. For instance, a company could be generating a set of scenarios looking out 5 years, and the Type A scenario would of course describe a logical future in which no significant change occurs. But this scenario might simply be describing how current stakeholders are applying increasing pressure and energy to maintain the status quo over that five year time frame. During that time, the frustration of stakeholders with grievances against the status quo could be rising quite fast, and the extension of the status quo could be provoking the formation of additional upstart stakeholders unsatisfied with the status quo, all of whom might be poised to provoke significant disruption *just beyond the time horizon of the scenario*.

In other words, just because a scenario looks unthreatening on the surface doesn't mean that there aren't important dynamics below the surface that you and your organization need to be watching.

It is in discussions like the one suggested above that the *experience* of developing the scenarios with a group of thoughtful and informed individuals helps to generate individual and collective insight into how and why things might change for your issue in the years ahead. Again, it's not about getting the end states "right"; it's about your organization developing insight into how and why the future will be different from today.

Conducting this futures stakeholder analysis puts you in a good position to now turn to exploring the specific implications of the scenarios for your organization's goals and strategies.

What Implications for Goals, Strategy, and Services?

Scenarios can of course be used to explore just about any question. For the purposes of the *4 Steps* model, we focus on just three areas: goals, strategy, and products/services. Here we are chiefly concerned with exploring how your organization's goals might need to change, how your current strategies would be impacted under each scenario, and how your portfolio of products and services would be altered.

- Goals: how would the scenarios impact your organization's strategic goals? Would they need to be refined, reduced or expanded, or discarded altogether? Importantly, change represents opportunity, and many scenarios present opportunities for an organization to establish compelling new goals to pursue: what new *aspirational* goals become possibilities under the scenarios?

- Strategy: related to the question of Goals but also potentially a distinct question, how would each scenario impact your current strategies? Would they become easier to execute, more difficult, or would they need to be completely overhauled? What new strategies might become possible or necessary?

- Products and Services: again, related to the preceding questions, how would the scenarios impact your portfolio of products and services? What new opportunities for innovation might the scenarios present? How will new customer groups, changing customer preferences, new technologies, and altered competitive landscapes shrink old market spaces while opening up new market opportunities?

Once again, the scenarios can be used to explore any number of possible questions, with the three above being merely the ones we've included as defaults in the *4 Steps* model. In the course of actually exploring the implications of your scenarios you should certainly consider additional questions to ask.

Early Warning and Indicators

Finally, we want to look at developing a set of indicators that would presage each of your scenarios. Commonly referred to as "early indicators," these are the signs your organization would use to anticipate one or more of the scenarios coming to pass. Indicators can take the form of hypothetical news headlines, specific developments of some type (such as new technologies coming on market, competitors making certain moves, or specific individuals taking office or positions of authority), or thresholds for trends and other quantitative metrics.

Generally, organizations use these indicators in conjunction with some form of internal, ongoing environmental scanning or monitoring function. An in-house team would continuously scan for these signs in the environment, alerting the rest of the organization when one or more were found, which would trigger discussions informed by the preceding foresight work. Again, the point is not to try to get the future right, but rather to think through logical possible changes ahead of time and then to recognize when those types of changes may be occurring.

Sample Indicators:
- Well-known regulatory hawk appointed to new position
- Competitors acquiring new emerging technology
- Sudden fall in critical supply prices
- California (often a leader) adopting a new policy
- Spokespersons issuing more dramatic rhetoric

A Note on Scenario Format and Presentation
Scenarios are fundamentally *stories* about potential change. As stories, it is important that you try to maximize their impact, and one of the most important ways of doing that is to think of them as stories (rather than dry, antiseptic forecasts) and to give some real thought to *how* they are formatted and communicated. Scenarios are most typically developed as written narratives, ranging from a couple of paragraphs to ten pages of detailed exposition. The exact length and detail is entirely dependent on your audience, but such text-based scenarios represent only one option. Alternative formats can include video, live-action skits (not kidding), manga, poster visualizations – basically through whatever medium (and combination of media) for which you have the time, bandwidth, and needs for your particular audience.

The important point is to communicate the scenarios in the most compelling format possible for your intended audience. You want the audience to quickly and easily engage the scenarios and for the scenarios to have the greatest chance of changing the way they think about the future of your issue.

Tool for the Futures: Scenarios
As mentioned earlier, scenarios are a workhorse tool for professional futurists. In fact, in various forms, most professionals of all stripes employ scenarios to some extent. In their simplest form, they are "what if" discussions or thought experiments. Sometimes they are the different outcomes from a model in a spreadsheet when we play with the variables to create different "scenarios." What distinguishes scenarios developed through a good foresight or futures research process from most common "what if" thinking and contingency planning is the very intentional structure we apply in forecasting challenging possibilities. In this way futures scenarios are not simply what-ifs taken off the tops of our heads. Rather, we are trying to be rigorous about challenging

assumptions about how the future might unfold and what might really be the range of future possibilities.

Main exercise

For this exercise you're going to be using Worksheet 3, which is built around the four scenario Types we just discussed. It will also be helpful to keep the Disruption Pyramid handy as a reference, since each scenario Type *generally* demonstrates different scales of disruption to your issue or organization.

Step 1: define your focal issue. Now is the time you need to decide on what really is the question you are asking about the future. What do you really need to explore? Don't forget to think about scope and timeframe, which will help narrow the topic.

Step 2: assemble all of the Historical Drivers, New Sources of change, and Stabilities identified earlier (and captured on Worksheets 1 and 2). Remember, you will need these as the core building blocks for the scenarios.

Step 3: assign Drivers, New Sources, and Stabilities to each of the scenarios. This is your first meaty activity and you will be filling in column 1 on the worksheet. Each scenario Type represents a different pattern of change, and this activity asks you (and your fellow participants, of course), "what combination of Historical Drivers, New Sources of change, and Stabilities would need to occur in order for the scenario's pattern to take form?" For example, in Type A scenarios, you need to put together the combination of building blocks that might logically produce continuity, where the only real disruption to your organization occurs at the top level of the Disruption Pyramid. Take your time here and have good, rich conversations.

Step 4: outline the scenarios. Moving to columns 2 – 4, you're now going to start sketching out each scenario. Here we're going to use the 3-layered approach we used when exploring the Past: daily experience, systems, and values. Based on: a) the scenario Type and its common plotline, and; b) the Historical Drivers, New Sources of change, and Stabilities you've already selected for each scenario, you're going to think about and discuss what the future would look like. What would daily experience actually look like? Which systems would be different (and how) and which would be the same? How would values and worldviews have shifted (or persisted)?

This is really the heart of the scenario process, so be sure to spend the most time right here. Working within the basic boundaries of each scenario's Type, how and why would things change? Reflect on the powerful forces for change represented by the Historical Drivers, all of them pushing on the status quo. Think about the possibilities so strongly suggested by the New Sources of change. Look over the Stabilities and ask yourself how strong they would be given each scenario Type. How then would all of these things interact? Keep in mind that few things change in nice, predictable, linear ways for very long; fusions and mash-ups of drivers and forces create unexpected opportunities, with the result of bending (and sometimes breaking) trend lines. In these conversations, push each other, challenge each other, and above all have fun!

Step 5: name the scenarios. Your final – and usually fun – task is to come up with a memorable and descriptive name for each scenario. It will help subsequent readers and audience members if the names quickly and vividly communicate the nature or "vibe" of the scenarios. What titles would make others really want to read the scenarios? It can also be useful to follow a theme for all of them, such as sticking to nature metaphors or using classic movie titles. The sky's the limit, so indulge your inner movie studio marketing exec!

Scenarios in Action: Global Scenarios for a Fortune 50
As mentioned previously in the "Emerging Issues Analysis in Action" case on page 24, a global food and beverage company commissioned a large, multifaceted foresight project involving several integrated steps. The step described previously – emerging issues analysis – fed directly into a scenario project that developed a set of original scenario forecasts about the global landscape. The purpose of the scenarios was to help the research divisions identify new technologies and emerging challenges they might get tasked with addressing as the future unfolded and the company's leaders called for solutions.

Thus, the client wanted to use scenarios to explore the complex and uncertain global landscapes they knew they would face in the mid- to long-term future. Drawing heavily on the preceding emerging issues work, our team designed and ran a series of scenario workshops over the course of six months. The workshops engaged dozens of scientists and researchers in describing and exploring some of the major, emerging issues that might confront the company over the next several years, examining in detail how current and future dynamics might interact with many of the trends and emerging issues. The scenarios that resulted presented a range of futures that were challenging yet full of potential opportunities for the client.

The scenarios proved to be a very valuable effort, leading the client to identify a number of lines of research to pursue, and focusing the company on some key long-term value shifts among customers and external stakeholders. The scenario work was later reviewed by the CEO of the company as the internal exemplar of foresight work, and the material was continually presented to internal audiences for the next couple of years. The foresight work also provided a much-appreciated planning reference for internal stakeholders.

Tool for the Futures: Scenario Implications
Scenario "implications" is really a collection of different frameworks and questions for exploring what the scenarios mean for your issue.

Main exercise

This exercise will use Worksheet 4 to help you conduct a futures stakeholder analysis, and to explore the implications of each scenario on your strategy and services. Note that, for this exercise you will be using a separate copy of Worksheet 4 for each scenario; in the end you should have four completed Implications worksheets.

Step 1: *Reacting*. This is the futures stakeholder analysis. Identify the key current stakeholders according to how they would react to the changes in each scenario, and then identify what they might do. Next, identify any logical future stakeholders to emerge in the scenario and what actions they might take. And don't forget that possible future stakeholders could include new types of competitors...

Step 2: *Assessing*. First, how would your organization's goals be impacted in each scenario? Next, wind tunnel your existing or proposed strategy through each scenario. How would they fare? Given the implications to your goals and current strategy, what new strategies might be possible or advisable? Finally, what changes to your organization's products and services might be necessary or possible? How would you need to – and how would you want to – alter your organization's product portfolio?

Throughout this step remember to refer back up to the futures stakeholder analysis to consider what you wrote there. It also helps to recall the general level of disruption (Disruption Pyramid) suggested by the scenario Type. When exploring the implications of a Type A (continuity) scenario, for instance, double check things if you find you (or your group) listing a bunch of huge changes needed for your organization's goals. In contrast, if the only implications people are exploring for a Type D (abrupt change) scenario are some minor changes to the product portfolio, that also might require a time out for regrouping.

Step 3: *Monitoring*. The final activity under Scenario Implications is to identify potential early indicators for each scenario. The easiest way to approach this is to think about the news headlines you would expect to read if a particular scenario was actually coming to pass. Early indicators can, of course, be a wide variety of things, from patent filings to new tech investments to public hearings. Jot down four or five for each scenario.

SCENARIOS

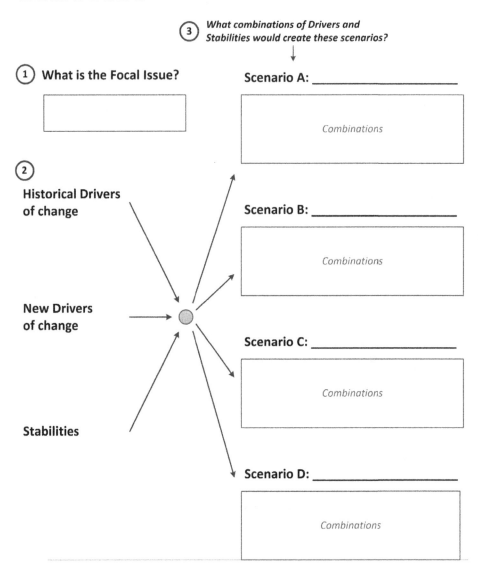

③ What combinations of Drivers and
   Stabilities would create these scenarios?

① What is the Focal Issue?

②
Historical Drivers
of change

New Drivers
of change

Stabilities

Scenario A: _____

Combinations

Scenario B: _____

Combinations

Scenario C: _____

Combinations

Scenario D: _____

Combinations

4 Steps to the Future Worksheet 3

(4) *What would the resulting scenarios look like?*
Describe how life is different at each level.

Daily Experience	Systems	Values

Daily Experience	Systems	Values

Daily Experience	Systems	Values

Daily Experience	Systems	Values

STEP 3: FUTURES

SCENARIO IMPLICATIONS   *4 Steps to the Future* Worksheet 4

(one per scenario)

Scenario: _____

(1) Reacting

There are three different basic reactions to the prospect of change: those who want to resist the changes; those who accept that change is coming and want to channel it according to their values; and those who want to accelerate or amplify the changes. How would various stakeholders respond to this scenario? In this scenario, who becomes an ally and who becomes a policy or strategy competitor?

Resistors	*Channelers*	*Accelerators*
Current	Current	Current
Future	Future	Future

(2) Assessing

What new products or markets open up to you in this scenario? What new strategies would be successful? How would existing or proposed strategies fair in this scenario?

Goals	**Strategies**	**Products/Services**
	Wind tunnel existing or proposed strategy	
	Ideas for new strategy	

(3) Monitoring

What headlines would tell you the world was heading in this direction?

Now just to recap at this point, so far you should have a clear focal issue for your futures work, four original scenarios, and a set of strategic implications from those scenarios. Reviewing things up to this point, we have:

- Change and Disruption
  - Types of Change
    - Continuity
    - Incremental
    - Abrupt
  - Disruption Pyramid
- Scenarios
  - Focal Issue
  - Scenario Types
    - Type A: continuity
    - Type B: incremental change, low disruption
    - Type C: incremental change, high disruption
    - Type D: abrupt
- Implications
  - Stakeholder Reactions
  - Impact on Goals, Strategies, and Services
  - Early Warning and Indicators

Now, let's take a quick breather while we use the image below to see where we are in the 4 Steps process and the kinds of thinking and the exercises we've gone over so far.

PAST	PRESENT	FUTURES	ASPIRATION
Recognizing patterns, cycles, and chance in your history.	Looking for historical forces at work, new changes, and forces against change	Exploring the futures you might face given the forces at work and patterns of change.	
☐ Layered Timeline	☐ Emerging Issues	☐ Scenarios	

Aspiration

The fourth and final step in the *4 Steps* model is to draw upon all of the insight and foresight generated in the preceding three steps (Past, Present, and Futures) and turn towards another single, deceptively simple question: "What future do you *want* to see happen?

In Aspiration we are leaving behind the questions of what has happened and what might happen and focusing fully on the question of what you (and your organization) want to see happen. This is the realm of what professional futurists call "preferred futures," and it is all about developing an inspiring vision towards which the organization strives.

Preferred Futures
Now, when most people hear the term "vision" in an organizational setting, the word conjures up notions of "happy-happy-joy-joy" statements about the future, wherein everything is rosy and all of our problems have been solved. If that makes you uncomfortable or just downright scares you off, then let me reassure you that "preferred futures" don't have to take such an extreme form. From a preferred futures perspective, working on vision – and the goals that have to be linked to it – is about aspiration and inspiration rather than simple blissful thinking. For example, the following is Vision Foresight Strategy's definition of "vision":

> *"An articulation of the organization's preferred future, informed by purpose, foresight, and aspiration."*

In this sense Vision is far less about wishful thinking and much more about using foresight to rethink the impact we want the organization to have in the world. Foresight helps to anticipate challenges, but it also helps to broaden our understanding of what's possible in the future, and that is what is really at play here in Step 4.

(Re)formulating Vision
Just about every single one of us carries within our heads (or our hearts) an image, however hazy, about the future we'd *like* to see. To drive home a key point, one of the most important applications of foresight work is to inform this image of the future, this image of our *preferred future*. All of the foresight work that is conducted should deepen our understanding of how and why things can change and broaden our view of what is actually possible. The foresight work takes us out of our daily, narrow domain and operational expertise to see a much broader landscape of change so that we can really rethink where we'd like to go.

The Content
What should a vision contain? Well, just about anything you need it to in order to communicate your preferred future to others. Having said that, there are certainly ways of

approaching preferred futures that can help you and your organization identify what is most important to your vision and communicate those elements to the world.

To start, it's helpful to think in terms of three concentric rings. As illustrated in figure 9, below, we can think about your organization as nested within larger contexts. The innermost ring is, of course, your organization and your staff. The middle ring represents your various direct stakeholders, of which your customers – those stakeholders for which you are specifically trying to develop products and services – are the critical and defining group. The outer ring represents the broader community(ies) in which your organization and its customers exist.

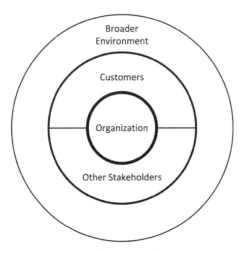

Figure 9: Context for Vision

Referencing this figure, we can ask, in which of these rings should your organization's vision sit? Many, many organizations have had vision statements that described their preferred future almost entirely in terms of the innermost ring; these visions were about *them*. Other organizations have had visions that talk about the (better) future of their customers, how the lives of their customers will be different and better in the future. And finally, still other organizations have had preferred futures that describe how the broader world will be better and more desirable for everyone.

None of these is necessarily the best choice, but we would offer that visions that focus either on how customers or how the broader community will be improved in the future are generally much more inspiring and galvanizing. And we do want visions to be inspiring, which is why we encourage you to ask yourself, "At what level should our vision exist in order to have the most resonance and inspiration for our staff and stakeholders?"

Generally, we advise clients to approach preferred futures by thinking about the lives of their customers, but the best choice is always dependent on the individual context for your organization. A company just starting to emerge from a very difficult and destabilizing history may really need a vision of how it can and will be a much better and stronger organization in the future, while a nonprofit focused on changing the priorities and practices of natural resource industries might be best inspired by a broad, global vision of a cleaner and more sustainable world.

Now, to return to the earlier definition of "vision" for just a minute, a vision as we define it is informed by three key things: purpose, foresight, and aspiration. We've spent most of this book walking through some simple steps for developing the foresight part, but we haven't yet touched on the other two, namely purpose and aspiration. So, let's take a very quick look at what can go into purpose and aspiration.

Purpose seems like an easy one, given that the word itself is synonymous with common organizational components like "mission." Indeed, whenever we work on preferred futures, we want to look back to the organization's founding purpose and its formal mission statement, if it has one. These are key touchstones that we want to, well, reach back and touch right now. *Why* was the organization started? What drove its initial work? What problem/challenge/opportunity was it trying to address?

In addition to looking at those foundational components, in talking about purpose we also want to spend some time thinking about the organization's history (different than the history of your issue from the Past, though they might well overlap). What challenges has it faced and overcome? How and why did it overcome them? What are the celebrated successes in the organization's history? What are its strengths? These may well be things that we want to perpetuate into the future.

Finally, aspiration is about what we want to accomplish, what we want to become. Whenever you've read about "stretch goals" or "audacious goals," they were talking about aspiration. If there's a dream element to developing preferred futures, then it's right here. What inspiration strikes us after having considered both the organization's purpose as well as the foresight we've developed? What might be possible in the future? What future would truly inspire people? If there's ever a time to dream big in foresight work, it is absolutely right here!

Just to help you a bit, below are a couple of examples of well-crafted and compelling preferred futures. You might even be familiar with them...

President John F. Kennedy's Moon Speech at Rice Stadium:

"There is no strife, no prejudice, no national conflict in outer space as yet. Its hazards are hostile to us all. Its conquest deserves the best of all mankind, and its opportunity for peaceful cooperation many never come again. But why, some say, the moon? Why choose this as our goal? And they may well ask why climb the highest mountain? Why, 35 years ago, fly the Atlantic? Why does Rice play Texas?

We choose to go to the moon. We choose to go to the moon in this decade and do the other things, not because they are easy, but because they are hard, because that goal will serve to organize and measure the best of our energies and skills, because that challenge is one that we are willing to accept, one we are unwilling to postpone, and one which we intend to win, and the others, too."

Institute for Alternative Futures:

IAF opens eyes, hearts and minds to alternative futures showing that aspiration is powerful and enduring. We partner with individuals, communities and organizations worldwide to look over the horizon so that their decisions today are accountable to tomorrow. IAF helps to create equitable, sustainable futures shaped by kindness, wisdom and foresight. Our work and our lives embody this hope for preferred futures.

The Format
OK, but what should all of this look like? Well, as with the discussion above about the content of preferred futures, there's really no one right way to pull this all together. For simplicity sake, the *4 Steps* model just has you develop a short bulleted list of descriptors. Well, that's for simplicity but also because in the model here we're more concerned with helping you focus on the content of your preferred future and less on the finer points of formatting.

The most important issue is, what do you *see* when you imagine your preferred future? That's what we really want to capture in creating preferred futures. In a very real sense, we ultimately want people to share some of the same imagery, to "be on the same page" as it were, with the organization's preferred future. "Vision statements" have often been written as values statements, but one of the dangers of talking solely in terms of value statements or sentiments is that people will see many different things when someone, say, invokes the term "care for the environment." Focusing on more concrete imagery helps to eliminate this problem.

Like scenarios (which are about *possible* futures), visions can be captured through text, through graphics, and anything more artistic and engaging. The important point is always to try to match the medium to the audience, and to the organization itself. A venerable and serious-minded think tank might not be the best audience for a vision for the future expressed through interpretive dance; while a community organization focused on revitalizing neighborhood youth programs might not get that much out of a two line vision statement.

Tool for Aspiration: Visioning
Over the years there have been many approaches to the activity generically called "visioning," in which a group develops a statement about what they want their future to look like. Community facilitators, corporate consultants, and urban planners have all developed different approaches to eliciting from people their individual preferences for the future and for blending those preferences together to produce a singular shared vision. No one approach is the "best" approach; rather like a lot of planning and foresight work, the best approach is always judged within your particular context.

The *4 Steps* model is designed for those times when you don't have a lot of time and/or resources with which to conduct your organization's foresight work, yet still want to apply some structure and critical thinking. In this context, visioning is not a standalone exercise in the *4 Steps* model and is intended to be part of a larger 1 ½ to 2-day workshop. The exercise outlined below is therefore designed to follow after – and draw upon – the Past, Present, and Futures exercises that were introduced earlier in this book.

Main exercise

This exercise will use Worksheet 5 and will ask you to refer back to just about all of the previous worksheets.

Step 1: list up to five of the most important strengths and the most meaningful successes in your organization's history. Similar to the historical timeline exercise from the previous section on the Past, build a timeline of your organization's history and fill it in with past challenges, crises, and triumphs. What happened? How did the organization pull through? On what skills, attitudes, and strengths did the organization rely to pull it through?

Step 2: list the five most important characteristics of the present. In what key ways would you describe it? Keep in mind that you're talking about it in terms of your organization. In fact, try thinking about it less in terms of your organization itself and more in terms of its customers. What would be the five most important characteristics you would share with a friend or outsider to really give them a mental image of what the present is like? Think about experiences, challenges, and other aspects of the present that generate need. With what do people struggle? What constraints keep better outcomes from emerging? What definitions, anxieties, and fears are holding folks back? Write down a couple of descriptors relating to the Broader Industry/Community, a couple related to your customers, and at least a couple related more directly to your organization.

Step 3: now you want to refer back to your previous work with the *4 Steps* model and consciously draw upon the foresight you've been developing. Looking back at Worksheet 2, recall the ways in which things are changing and can change. Think about some of those amazing, even inspiring, emerging issues and technologies. Go back to the scenarios captured on Worksheet 3 and look for ways in which things changed that you would actually like to see happen. Look across your Worksheet 4s for ideas on innovative new products and services and for new strategies. Write down a couple of insights relating to the Broader Industry/Community, a couple related to your customers, and at least a couple more directly to your organization.

Step 4: now, visualize the present *passing through* that foresight layer in the middle of the worksheet: what might the future look like on the other side? How might the future be different from the present, and for the better? What things could be achieved? Most importantly, how will the lives of your customers be improved in ways they would appreciate? These ideas are what you want to capture in a new list of the five most important characteristics that you would use to describe a *better future*.

Visioning in Action: Crafting a Statewide Vision for a Sustainable Future

As the 21st century dawned, "sustainability" came to the fore as one of the most widely talked about values in communities, on campuses, and in boardrooms. We were privileged to be part of the formation of a successful and long-lasting non-profit organization that first brought together Generation X and then galvanized Millennials with the idea of building a more just and sustainable future. In the earliest days of the organization – indeed, before it even was a formal organization – we were asked to guide the founders through a foresight and visioning process to develop a new vision for the long-term future of their state. This vision was critical to them as it was to set the tone and establish the basic direction of the future organization's efforts.

The project was designed around three successive workshops, involving young professionals, academics, and community activists in broad ranging discussions about the future. The workshops provided inspiring talks by esteemed and supportive local leaders, framed discussions about key trends and emerging issues, developed a set of original scenarios, and culminated in a new, shared vision for the future of the state. The discussions across these three workshops were deep, challenging, and at times tense, as the participants were forced to examine each other's and their own assumptions about the future and about the group's values.

Despite the challenging conversation – or perhaps because of it – the visioning process enabled the group to develop a clear and articulate vision of their preferred future that was informed by both foresight and aspiration. Because the process required the participants to be articulate in their preferences and because it allowed for the group to address differences and misunderstandings, the resulting vision was much clearer for the group and founded on a truly shared understanding of the values and trade-offs it entailed. With this vision in place, the organization rapidly gained momentum and support, ultimately receiving significant funding and becoming one of the most recognizable forces for positive change in its state.

Now, let's take a quick breather while we use the image below to see where we are in the 4 Steps process and the kinds of thinking and the exercises we've gone over so far.

PAST	PRESENT	FUTURES	ASPIRATION
Recognizing patterns, cycles, and chance in your history.	Looking for historical forces at work, new changes, and forces against change	Exploring the futures you might face given the forces at work and patterns of change.	Drawing upon values, strengths, and foresight to articulate the future you want to see.
☐ Layered Timeline	☐ Emerging Issues Analysis	☐ Scenarios ☐ Scenario Implications	☐ Visioning

VISIONING

Vision: *"An articulation of the organization's preferred future, informed by purpose, foresight, and aspiration."*

(2) The Present:
List the five most important characteristics of the present.

1.

2.

3.

4.

5.

The present,

passing through the foresight layer...

(3) Foresight:
Write down some of t captured in Workshee

1.

2.

3.

4.

5.

(1) Strengths & Successes:
List the five most important strengths from your organization's history to carry into the future.

1.

2.

3.

4.

5.

Visualizing Your Prefe

Use this space to draw your diagrams, pasted magazine

4 Steps to the Future **Worksheet 5**

he insights
:ts 1 – 4.

④ **Your Preferred Future:**
List five of the most important
characteristics of a better future.

1.

...could become a *better* future.   2.

3.

4.

5.

:rred Futures

preferred future. Stick figures, icons,
clippings, or panoramic drawings!

STEP 4: ASPIRATION

Conclusion

Now see, that didn't take very long, did it?

We certainly hope it didn't, because of all people we can absolutely appreciate how valuable is time and we know you and your organization are trying to make the best use of yours.

The *4 Steps to the Future* model was designed to be a quick and clean guide to producing foresight, something that just about anyone, in any size organization could use right out of the box. Good foresight work, no matter how in depth or exhaustive always includes some element of all four of the *Model's* steps, and in this book we wanted to start you off with some of the basic questions that you should ask and some initial structure for answering them.

In many respects, futures thinking is just a particular type of critical thinking. It's just unfortunate that the vast majority of us are never formally taught how to do it. And while there's potentially a lot of sophistication that can go into futures thinking and foresight work, even a few basic questions and process points can go a long way to creating informed and critical discussions within organizations. The *4 Steps* model tries to do this for you using a nice, linear process producing a series of tangible outputs.

And if, in the process of using the *4 Steps* model with your colleagues, you ever find yourself stuck, try going back to basics and just ask yourselves: why does change happen? And what does that mean in terms of the different possible, but logical futures your organization might face? And given those different possibilities, what should we be thinking about, planning for, and how do our *preferences* for the future change?

For those wanting to go deeper into futures thinking and foresight, there are a variety of resources out there for you to access. There are a few long-standing futures organizations and a number of futures studies and foresight journals, in addition to degreed programs around the world. A number of them are listed in Additional Resources and we, of course, would always be happy to help your organization with producing and learning to produce foresight.

And now, get back to the futures!

Glossary

Emerging Issue: any new technology under development, potential future public policy issue, or new concept or idea that might be fringe thinking now but which *could* mature and develop into the mainstream; usually encountered as "weak signals" in the present.

Forecast: a statement about the future intended to be logical, though not necessarily accurate (see Prediction); to use formal theories and rules to anticipate change.

Foresight: insight into how and why the future may be different from the present.

Futures: the contemplation, exploration, description, and anticipation of potential change (for contrast, see History).

Futures Studies: an academic field concerned with understanding and anticipating change in society.

Futures Wheel: a common and easy-to-learn visual method for futures research in which the first, second, and third order impacts of an emerging issue or future scenario are explored.

History: a description of change (Karl Popper)

Horizon Scanning: Also known as environmental scanning, a process of skimming a wide variety and high volume of information sources in order to identify signals of emerging change.

Intuitive Possibility: emerging issues with few or just a single data point, but their possibility is both logical and compelling.

Maturing Development: the most mature category of emerging issue; those possibilities for which there is a growing set of signals of change: research projects, commercial investment, increasing mention in articles and blogs, etc...

Mission: an organization's purpose, often articulated as a statement describing how the organization is configured to achieve its vision and thereby serve the needs of its customers.

Plan: a sequence of actions selected to attain an objective

Precognition: "clairvoyance related to an event or state not yet experienced"; to know beforehand.

Prediction: a statement about the future that is intended to be accurate.

Prophecy: a statement about an event about which you can do nothing (Karl Popper).

Scenario: a description of an alternative, possible future.

Strategy: a concept or theory for how, in a given context and employing a given set of resources and competencies, you expect to achieve your goals.

Strengthening Signal: emerging issues with fewer signals or anecdotes indicating their emergence than Maturing Developments, but still having a clear sense that there might "be something there."

Trend: a measurable change over time; historical.

Vision: an articulation of the preferred future of an organization, measurably vivid, informed by foresight, purpose, and aspiration.

Additional Resources

VFS Training Seminars

Vision Foresight Strategy offers training seminars in the *4 Steps to the Future* model as well as a variety of foresight training options to meet the needs of both smaller and larger organizations. Options range from increasing basic foresight "fluency" to deep dives into advanced futures research methods. Training options also run from single day courses to full 4-day programs.

Learn more at www.visionforesightstrategy.com.

Additional Reading

If you'd like to learn more about some of the concepts and methods presented in the *4 Steps* model, the following are some good resources for diving a little deeper into the field of futures studies and foresight development.

VFS Primer on Foresight. A quick walk through some of the important thinking and products of professional futurists producing foresight. Available for download from www.visionforesightstrategy.com.

Why Futures Studies? by Eleanora Masini. A great (and short) introduction to some of the philosophy and history of futures.

Foundations of Futures Studies, by Wendell Bell. A large two volume work on the history, methods, and issues in the field of futures studies.

Verge General Practice Framework

If you're interested in learning a bit more about the Verge General Practice Framework for futures research, then download the introductory slide deck on it from http://www.slideshare.net/richardl91/apf-2013-104 or visit the VFS publications page on www.visionforesightstrategy.com.

Futures Education

If you're so jazzed by what you read here that you want to look into formal futures education, then the following are the three universities in the United States where one can earn a degree in futures studies (go, you!):

- University of Houston (www.houstonfutures.org)
- University of Hawaii at Mānoa (www.futures.hawaii.edu)
- Regents University (www.regent.edu)

Professional Organizations

If you've already had training or a bit of career doing foresight in some fashion and would like to connect up with other experienced professionals, or if you're just looking to meet up with trained futurists at a future event, then check out the following professional futures organizations.

Association of Professional Futurists: a professional association for futurists, this organization was started in 2002 to provide trained, professional futurists with a formal space in which to share practice and promote professional excellence in futures thinking. www.apf.org.

World Future Society: probably the most well-known of these organizations to business and government, the World Future Society is primarily a North American organization that traditionally offered a gateway into the larger futures and foresight community. Best known among "lay" folks for their annual conference. www.wfs.org.

World Futures Studies Federation: the most academically-minded and socially-oriented of the organizations, the Federation is also the most global in its membership. The Federation was started by many of the first generation luminaries of the futures field, and continues to demonstrate the greatest concern for the long-term and systemic issues confronting human society today. www.wfsf.org.

Academic and Professional Journals
The following are a few of the better known journals explicitly focused on futures studies and foresight.

Foresight: an international journal concerned with the study of the future published by Emerald. www.emeraldgrouppublishing .com

Futures: an international journal concerned with medium and long-term futures, also covering methods of futures studies. www.journals.elsevier.com/futures.

Journal of Futures Studies: a quarterly journal concerned with futures studies. Published by Tamkang University Press on behalf of the Graduate Institute of Futures Studies. jfs.tku.edu.tw/.

World Future Review: a journal concerned with promoting public education and understanding of the methods and use of futures research, as well as the role of futures research in the larger context of decision-making. us.sagepub.com.

About Vision Foresight Strategy LLC

Vision Foresight Strategy LLC (VFS) is a Honolulu-based firm that provides foresight and strategic analysis services to senior organizational leaders operating in contexts of high complexity and high uncertainty. Drawing upon a global network of academically trained futurists, seasoned global executives, and experienced management consultants, VFS offers clients a spectrum of services that stretch from original forecasts and scenario projects to organizational foresight training to strategy development.

VFS' core expertise is the integration of formal futures studies methods with strategic thinking and strategy development. Client deliverables typically include trend and emerging issues analyses, original scenario forecasts, vision (preferred futures) development, strategy development workshops, and foresight skill development. Since the company's founding in 2001 it has participated in scenario projects for clients such as the US Army Logistics Command, the UK Government, PepsiCo, Grant Thornton UK, and numerous other organizations. VFS team members have conducted foresight, horizons scanning, scenario, and strategy work for a variety of clients and projects that include: Futurium (the European Union's experimental platform for crowdsourcing scanning and foresight for policy), US Pacific Command, the UK Defra Baseline Scan, the UK Foresight Programme, and the State Justice Institute.

About Richard A. K. Lum

Richard is an academically trained futurist and chief executive of Vision Foresight Strategy LLC, a foresight and strategic analysis firm based in Honolulu. His professional interests include the futures of governance, conflict and security, and industrialism.

Richard has worked with a wide variety of non-profit organizations, for-profit companies, and government agencies on foresight, strategy development, and strategic thinking. He has developed strategy for clients in industries as diverse as defense, education, healthcare, and insurance. He has helped organizations apply foresight and develop strategy for endeavors ranging from the restoration of ancient Hawaiian island land management divisions to crowdsourcing foresight development for the European Union to helping educators in the US anticipate the long term futures of learning.

Richard holds a PhD in Political Science from the futures studies program at the University of Hawai'i.

Appendix

The following pages include copies of the principles, ground rules, and habits presented on pages 3-6 as well as full-page versions of the five worksheets.

Digital copies of the worksheets in their full 11x17 inch format are available for download at www.visionforesightstrategy.com.

QUICK REFERENCE

PAST   PRESENT   FUTURES   ASPIRATION

Recognizing patterns, cycles, and chance in your history.

Looking for historical forces at work, new changes, and forces against change

Exploring the futures you might face given the forces at work and patterns of change.

Drawing upon values, strengths, and foresight to articulate the future you want to see.

☐ Layered Timeline

☐ Emerging Issues Analysis

☐ Scenarios
☐ Scenario Implications

☐ Visioning

4 Steps to the Future

1. Past
   a. How has [your issue] changed over the last several years?
   b. Why did those changes happen?
2. Present
   a. Which of those forces are at work again?
   b. What new sources of change?
3. Futures
   a. What are the logical alternative futures for [your issue]?
   b. What are the opportunities or threats?
   c. Who will resist, channel, or accelerate change?
4. Aspiration
   a. What new goals?
   b. What new vision?

Principles

- The future does not exist (we're all helping to create it)
- There are many possible futures
- Those futures are constantly in flux

Everyday Habits

A. Expose yourself to lots of stuff

B. Break out of bounds

C. Think (and take notes) visually

D. Keep asking *why?*

E. Prompt others to reconsider *what if?*

Ground Rules for the *4 Steps*

1. Stop trying to hit the bull's-eye

2. Keep numbers in their place

3. Collect lots of stuff

4. Be ruthless with expectations

5. Take everyone's input

6. Do this every year

7. In fact, do a little bit of this all the time

PRINCIPLES, HABITS, AND RULES

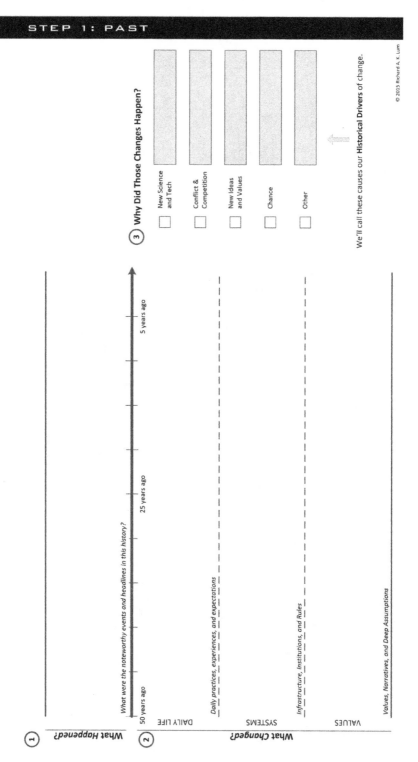

4 Steps to the Future Worksheet 1

STEP 1: PAST

HISTORICAL ANALYSIS

This is the first of five worksheets in the 4 Steps model. What happened in the past? What drove change?

① What Happened?

What were the noteworthy events and headlines in this history?

50 years ago   25 years ago   5 years ago

② What Changed?

DAILY LIFE — Daily practices, experiences, and expectations

SYSTEMS — Infrastructure, Institutions, and Rules

VALUES — Values, Narratives, and Deep Assumptions

③ Why Did Those Changes Happen?

☐ New Science and Tech
☐ Conflict & Competition
☐ New Ideas and Values
☐ Chance
☐ Other

We'll call these causes our **Historical Drivers** of change.

© 2015 Richard A. K. Lum

STEP 2: PRESENT

4 Steps to the Future Worksheet 2

The STEEP framework.

TRENDS, EMERGING ISSUES, AND STABILITIES

Together our Trends and Emerging issues are what we'll call our **New Drivers** of change.

1 Trends

What are some of the trends that are currently driving change? Identify both trends that are going up as well as those that are headed down.

Think about *counter* trends that are being provoked as a result of these initial trends.

Increasing Trends

Decreasing Trends

2 Counter Trends

Driving Change

3 Emerging Issues

What new ideas, issues, or technologies are below the radar now, but might mature into important drivers of change?

Snapshot of the Present

Forecast: when each issue will top the s-curve

Today   3 years   5 years   10 years   15 years   20 years   25 years

4 Stabilities

What things will slow or prevent change? We'll call these our **Stabilities**.

Common types of stability-enforcing things:

- Rules, customs, and traditions
- Physical or logistical constraints
- Patterns of behavior
- Powerful stakeholders or incumbents

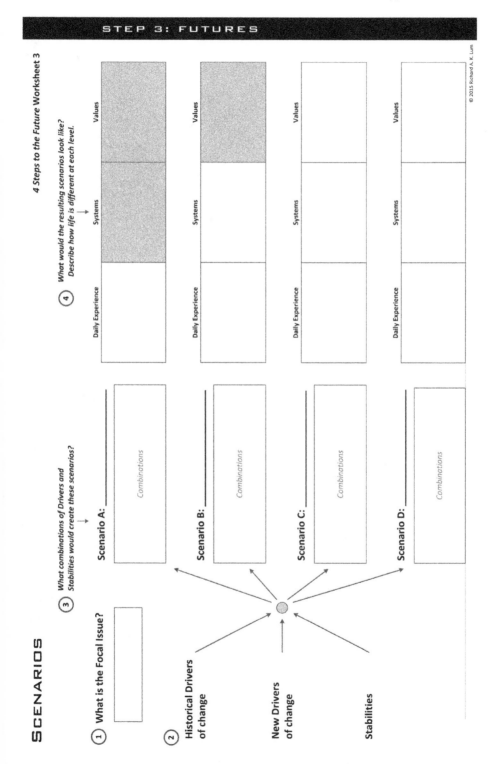

SCENARIO IMPLICATIONS

4 Steps to the Future **Worksheet 4**

(one per scenario)

Scenario: _____

(1) Reacting

There are three different basic reactions to the prospect of change: those who want to resist the changes; those who accept that change is coming and want to channel it according to their values; and those who want to accelerate or amplify the changes. How would various stakeholders respond to this scenario? In this scenario, who becomes an ally and who becomes a policy or strategy competitor?

Resistors	*Channelers*	*Accelerators*
Current	Current	Current
Future	Future	Future

(2) Assessing

What new products or markets open up to you in this scenario? What new strategies would be successful? How would existing or proposed strategies fair in this scenario?

Goals	**Strategies**	**Products/Services**
	Wind tunnel existing or proposed strategy	
	Ideas for new strategy	

(3) Monitoring

What headlines would tell you the world was heading in this direction?

© 2015 Richard A. K. Lum

4 Steps to the Future Worksheet 5

VISIONING

Vision: *"An articulation of the organization's preferred future, informed by purpose, foresight, and aspiration."*

② The Present:
List the five most important characteristics of the present.

1.

2.

3.

4.

5.

③ Foresight:
Write down some of the insights captured in Worksheets 1 – 4.

1.

2.

3.

4.

5.

④ Your Preferred Future:
List five of the most important characteristics of a better future.

1.

2.

3.

4.

5.

The present,

passing through the foresight layer...

...could become a *better* future.

① Strengths & Successes:
List the five most important strengths from your organization's history to carry into the future.

1.

2.

3.

4.

5.

Visualizing Your Preferred Futures

Use this space to draw your preferred future. Stick figures, icons, diagrams, pasted magazine clippings, or panoramic drawings!

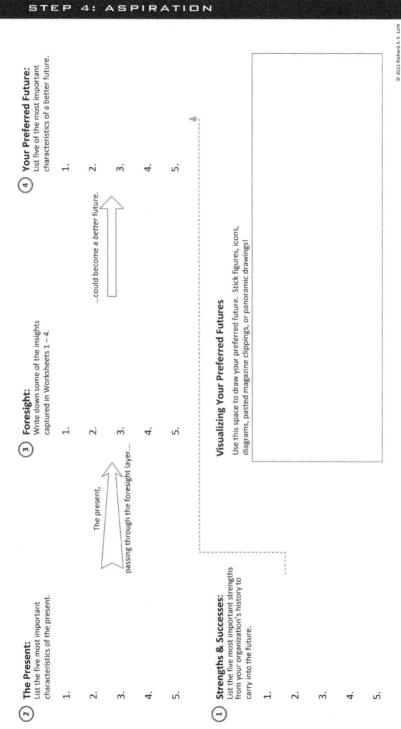

Index

- Criminalization - adverse impacts.

- Market over saturation in the race to legalization

- Company X - <u>CEO</u>
   of Company
     • Build brands
     • United.

core
← How to structure to capit- on the upside why ?
don't

- Societal + social paradigm
- Medicalization within progressive
- Federal nation
- Economics = locally grown supply-side =
    - Blaaa... let obsolete.
        .

- Lack of small business loans
    - Access to capital
- Counter - trends
    - States where they have made it legal but backlash against it.
    - Recreational users demand.
    - Slow or stall federal legalization.

- First order -
  - Toe-hold in the U.S.
  - Canadian producers
  - Global Markets
  - Privatizing

- Organizational

- Preferred scenario -

- Capitalize on the unrest
  (

CPSIA information can be obtained
at www.ICGtesting.com
Printed in the USA
BVHW030241240320
575821BV00001B/234